The Nine Lives of
Montezuma

The Nine Lives of Montezuma

Montezuma

MICHAEL MORPURGO

ILLUSTRATED BY MARGERY GILL

mammoth

First published in Great Britain 1980
by Kaye and Ward Ltd
Published 1992 by Mammoth
Reissued 1998 by Mammoth
an imprint of Egmont Children's Books Ltd
Michelin House, 81 Fulham Road, London SW3 6RB

Text copyright © 1980 Michael Morpurgo
Illustrations copyright © 1980 Margery Gill

The moral rights of the author, illustrator and cover illustrator
have been asserted.

ISBN 0 7497 1229 5

3 5 7 9 10 8 6 4

A CIP catalogue record for this title
is available from the British Library

Printed and bound in Great Britain
by Cox & Wyman Ltd, Reading, Berkshire

*For Kippe and Jack who
first warned me about cats*

The Beginning

The barn owl had been waiting for some time
high up in the rafters of the dutch barn. He was
a young barn owl and had not yet the patience
of an experienced adult. He had been hunting
for some months now, making slow, silent

sorties along the hedgerows, his eyes scanning the undergrowth for the sudden inexplicable movement that might betray the prey beneath. For hours he had waited perched among the elms surveying the darkness below before gliding out through the branches and swooping down, talons poised and primed for the kill. But too often his balance and timing still failed him. He would find himself taking off too early, allowing his quarry too much time to elude him. He had not yet perfected the technique of waiting for the right moment that all efficient hunters need if they are to make a good kill. Hunger gnawed at his stomach, concentrating his mind. He sat still on his perch like a white sentinel, and waited.

Far below him in a hollow between two bales of hay lay the old she-cat, stretched out to allow her young to suckle. One kitten was already dead and lay cold, damp and alone. The three survivors fought for their mother's milk, clambering over each other in blind hunger, probing for the wet warmth of a teat amongst the soft fur of her belly. She was aware that the owl was watching. She had seen him swoop in from the night and sit high above her, fold his wings back and settle down. She would have moved her kittens, had she had the time, but they had only just been born and she was too exhausted to move. Anyway, she knew that they were safe so long as she stayed with them. She lifted her head and glanced almost casually up at the owl above her. It was a waiting game, a stand-off; and she could wait as long as he would. She curled round and licked over her litter so that they tumbled from her mewing and pawing the air in a frantic effort to retrieve their feeding places. The she-cat cleaned them individually all over and then nudged them back so that they could feed again. She looked for a moment at the dead kitten and then stretched out and gave down her milk.

Dawn was filtering the darkness and the owl shifted perceptibly on his branch, uneasy now at the long wait. His patience had been tried for too long. His eyes blinked black, once, twice: and he lifted himself easily off the rafter, spreading his wings to begin the slow glide down towards the cat. Half in sleep she heard the rush of wind against his wings and was at once alert to the danger. She sprang up, shielding her young, and spitting defiance as the owl swooped down. She backed away, lifting her front paws to fend him off; but the owl had seen his chance, the undefended kitten lying apart and still in the corner of the hollow. He turned, wheeled powerfully and came in again his talons outstretched. He had but to choose the right angle of attack to avoid those unsheathed claws and the kill would be his. There was scarcely a hesitation in his flight as he plucked the dead kitten from the hay and swung away up over the bales and out into the grey of dawn, leaving behind the old she-cat still spitting her anger after him.

Her dead kitten had been her family's safe passage. Now there was time to move out of reach of intruders, deeper into the sanctuary of the haystack. One by one she picked up her kittens and carried them in her mouth down the hay stack and up into the old straw where the bales were less tightly packed and where some

bales had fallen apart. Finding a safe place took some time; but finally, with the first kitten in her mouth, she found a suitable burrow and squeezed her way in, depositing the kitten at the bottom. Then she went back for the others. This was the danger period when each of the kittens in turn had to be left, and the old she-cat ran and leapt again like a young cat. Perhaps the owl returning, a rat, or even another cat might come upon the kitten while she was gone. Only when the task was done and they were all three suckling her in their prickly new nest, did she feel safe.

Over the next few days, in the musty darkness of their new home the kittens' eyes began to unstick, and they had their first blurred impression of light. They were still too weak to explore and yearned only for the warmth and food that their mother provided. Secure now from the owl, the she-cat had begun leaving her litter for short periods. She had to feed herself if her litter was to survive. To start with it would be a matter of minutes only until she returned, but as the kittens grew and as time went on she took to wandering further afield to hunt, and she returned only when her hunger had been satisfied.

From the dead beech tree by the duck pond, the young barn owl had been watching her comings and goings much as a conspiring bank robber watches a security guard. Each evening after he had taken the dead kitten he had flown in and searched for the rest of the litter. That they were there he knew for certain, but he had not yet been able to locate them. This evening he waited for the she-cat to climb the hedge into the meadow and watched her as she padded into the trees beyond and vanished. Then he leapt down onto the wind and floated across into the barn.

The three kittens were still groping after the warmth of their mother, two of them silently; but the third was calling after his mother, his mewing turned to high-pitched wails of anxiety as he discovered she was gone. From his observation post near the roof the owl heard, registered, and blinked his round black eyes. He could not see them, but he had them pinpointed now. He would be back.

The spring had been late in coming and the animals on the farm were still indoors, still waiting for the land to dry and the grass to grow through. Each morning and evening the yearlings in the granary needed to be fed with hay and their bedding made up with straw. During the school holidays this was the boy's task whilst his father finished the milking and washed down the dairy.

It was evening and he was in the big hay-barn throwing down the bales of straw for the bedding when he came across the three kittens. They were alone, piled up in a heap that wriggled suddenly to life as he moved away the bale that had been the roof of their nest.

He was about to shout out to his father that old Kitty, the she-cat, had done it again; but he decided against it. His father would drown them in the pond as he had done many times before. His father liked to keep a tidy farm, and too many cats implied there might be too many mice and rats. One or two of them served a useful purpose; more than that and they were always under your feet and hanging around the back yard. The boy thought for a moment, and then replaced the bale purposefully. If they could stay there undiscovered for a week or so, then he knew his father would stay his hand even if they were found after that. His father would drown them only in the first week or so of life, before their eyes were properly open.

The boy always fed the pigs after milking and then went back indoors where his mother would have a hot cup of tea waiting for him. He pulled off his boots, threw his coat in a corner and flopped down in the big kitchen chair by the stove.

"Your father's been and gone," said his mother, pouring out the tea automatically.

"What's he gone out for? He'd just about finished up when I left."

"He came in for a sack."

"What for?" The boy tried his tea but it was too hot.

"That old cat has had kittens again," his mother said.

"You mean Kitty?" The boy knew what had happened but wanted to know how. The kittens had been well hidden. "Where did he find them?" he asked.

"He said you were one bale short on the straw. There wasn't enough for the yearlings." There was a hint of reproof in his mother's voice. "So he had to go back into the big barn and fetch one and he found them in under the bale he picked up."

"How many, Mum?"

"Didn't say, but that Kitty never produces less than three or four."

"In the pond? Is that where he will do it?"

"I expect so, dear; it usually is. Now drink your tea. It will get cold."

As the boy sipped his tea and warmed his hands on the cup, he began to wonder how his father, normally the gentlest man he knew, could bring himself to do it. And that led on to his wondering if he himself was really right to be a farmer. He loved to raise the animals and watch them grow, but he found the killing difficult to take. Of course he knew that all his stock ended up in the abattoir, but that after all was how they made their living. It was a part of the farming and he could accept it, just so long as someone else did the killing. He could never contemplate killing with his own bare hands, not so close that you can feel and hear the animal. Shooting was different; there was sport in that, and anyway killing with a gun at a distance was no problem to him.

His father was back. The boy heard him stamp his boots outside the door and waited for the usual comment about his coat.

"I see your coat's on the floor again," said his father whipping off his stiff flat hat and hanging it up. "By gad, you youngsters these days, you'll never learn."

He ignored his father. "Did you drown them, Dad?"

"All done," he said. "They were only just born. They wouldn't know anything about it."

"How many did she have, Dad?" the boy asked.

"Two. Just two this time. It's a business. I wish she'd go off and have them somewhere else. Silly old cat, she must know I've drowned more than half of the kittens she's ever had. You'd think she'd have the sense to go elsewhere. Any tea left in the pot?"

"Just two then, Dad? You didn't see any more?" His father shook his head. There had been three kittens, of that the boy was quite certain.

"That old cat won't miss them," said his mother. "Those we don't drown she deserts before they're properly weaned, and I know she eats them herself sometimes. She's a terrible mother; we ought to have had her fixed years ago. Would've saved all this trouble."

The boy stood up, mumbled something about leaving his torch behind in the pigs' house, slipped his boots on and went out.

The lone kitten had managed to scramble about back up onto the bale which was his home. In a desperate search for his absent mother he had toppled off the bale and fallen into a deep crevasse between the bales below; and it was that that had saved his life. Stumbling about in the darkness he searched now for the warmth of his mother and cried out for her. He lifted his nose scenting the night air and explored every corner of his home. His family had gone, and the plaintive mewing turned to a cry of panic as the realisation that he was alone took hold of him.

It was this sharp cry that attracted the white

owl perched in the beech tree by the pond. He
had been watching a water vole that kept pushing its head out of its hole in the muddy bank
by the stump of an old alder tree. He was waiting
for it to emerge, but had the feeling that it might
never happen. The cry from the barn was a
reminder to him. He needed no further invitation. He knew the place and guessed from the
fear in the cry that the kittens were alone. He
circled the barn and came in to perch on the
rafter just above the nest. Even before he landed
he had spied the kitten alone and exposed, groping its way across the bale. The great black eyes
focused and blinked. His head turned on his neck
searching out the barn for the she-cat. But there
was no sign of her. He paused momentarily to
be sure and then lifted his wings and fell through
the air, his legs outstretched, his talons spread.

From her hunting ground by the grain store,
the old she-cat had heard her kitten. The hunting
had been poor, and she knew she had left her
kittens for too long. She came in under the big
barn doors just as the owl took off. Within the
space of a second she was by her kitten and
standing her ground. The owl wheeled away
only feet above the squirming kitten, shocked at
the sudden intrusion; but he came back again
with renewed fury. He had been certain of a kill.
Three more times he came in, his talons almost

touching the she-cat's paws, but the last time he saw the anger and ferocity in her eyes and he feared it. He knew the game was lost and with long powerful strokes of his great white wings he soared out of the barn and back up into the beech tree. There he snapped his beak in frustration and settled down to wait for a chance at his alternative kill, the water vole. But his vigil was disturbed by the approach of hurried footsteps across the yard and the dancing beam of a torch. He gave up in disgust and flew off, a silent white ghost in the night.

The boy pulled open the big barn door and shone his torch up at the place where he had seen the kittens. The she-cat was there and she was not alone. He approached slowly, climbing over the bales up towards her. Kitty blinked in the light and swallowed nervously. "It's only me, Kitty. Won't hurt you, you know that." He spoke in caressing tones until he could reach out and stroke her with his hand. Almost hidden underneath her and already suckling he found the surviving kitten, ginger with a white patch on his throat.

"I've a good mind to take him into care," the boy said, still stroking the she-cat. "You've already lost at least two, and I shouldn't wonder if you've eaten one or two yourself. You take care of him, you hear. He deserves to survive,

that one does. What with you for a mother, and my father with his sack, he must be some cat to have survived; but he's only got eight more lives you know. Best move him out of here; if my Dad finds him here he'll go the same way as the other two. Understand?''

The boy left them in the barn and made his way home across the yard. It was beginning to rain and the raindrops slanted across the beam of his torch. He was singing inside.

The Second Life

There are places on a farm where no one ever goes and it was to one of these that the she-cat carried her last surviving kitten. There was an old cob granary in one corner of the farmyard, so old and battered that it appeared almost to grow out of the stones of the yard. The only hint that it might have been man-made was the decaying corrugated iron roof that had replaced the thatch some years before. The building was used now to house the yearling cattle in winter, but the attic room above had been disused as long as anyone could remember. The floorboards were rotten and loose, and the joists they rested on would no longer stand the weight of a man. Here a cat could live undisturbed, and here the she-cat came with her kitten to live.

Times were busy on the farm. The spring was late in coming and when the weather finally turned dry the ploughing had to take priority if the barley was to be tilled in time. At weekends the boy was left to manage most of the farm work on his own while his father rode out every morning, the plough hitched to the tractor, his lunch in his bag; and he came home only when the light failed in the evening. The boy worked well on his own, he had been well tutored by his father and had already acquired the farmer's knack of working at a regular, unhurried pace, of moving amongst the stock with a calm confidence so that the animals barely seemed to notice he was there.

It was a warm misty morning in early April when he opened the gate and drove the yearlings out to grass for the first time in their lives. He looked on as they stepped gingerly in the softness of the grass, standing huddled together in the gateway. None of them seemed to want to take the step out onto the strange green ocean of the meadow. Then first one and then another sensed their new freedom, tossed their heads and ran out kicking up their legs in delight and leaping like lambs. The boy leant on the gate and enjoyed it, before turning back to the granary, to the task of cleaning out the bed of dung that had built up over the winter. He did not relish it.

He had filled the spreader for the first time and was sitting on the cold stone water trough resting, when he heard something moving on the ceiling above him. He stood up to listen again. There was no sound at first and then he heard a faint rustle and squeaking. "Rats," he thought and picked up the scoop to begin again. Until this moment the boy had not given another thought to the ginger kitten he had found some weeks before in the big barn, but as he shovelled away under the hay racks it came to him that the squeaking he had heard was perhaps more that of a kitten than a rat.

He climbed the granite steps that led up the side of the granary to the attic door. It was dark inside, the only window being covered with a sack. He knew the floor was dangerous and went down on all fours testing the soundness of each board as he crawled round the wall towards the window. As he reached up and pulled away the sack, he heard the sound again, louder this time and more urgent. He peered across the small room and called out in that language that people seem to think cats understand better. "Puss, puss, puss, kitty, kitty, kitty. Where are you, kitty?" There was no response and he could see nothing, so he began to feel his way forward across the middle of the floor. He felt the joists spring under him and there was an ominous cracking as the wood adjusted to his weight. He stopped, waiting for the floor to be still again, and then he inched his way forward. He found the kitten lying behind a pile of disintegrating corn sacks. There was no resistance when he picked him up, the kitten opened his mouth to voice his objection but was too feeble now to utter any sound. He lay limp in the boy's hands.

He could not be sure it was the same kitten until he had made the hazardous journey around the walls and back to the door. Once outside in the light it was clear that this was indeed the kitten he remembered, the ginger tom with a white patch on his throat that extended from the chin to his chest. The kitten had grown. Whereas before there had been no perceptible neck, his head seemed now to have distanced itself from the body; but the body itself was emaciated and wasted. Through the cold fur the boy could feel only the sharpness of bones. As if awakened by the light the kitten tensed himself and made to escape, his claws sinking into the boy's wrist; but there was no stamina in the effort. "There's life in you yet then, old son," said the boy as he cradled the kitten carefully in his hands and made his way back across the yard towards the house.

"Best treat him like an orphan lamb," said his mother. "He's half dead with cold and by the looks of him near starved to death. That Kitty has deserted him. I don't know how she can do it. She'll fight for her young, protect them, raise them and leave them half-weaned." She bent down and opened the bottom oven door of the stove. This was where they warmed the premature lambs born out in the cold of night and brought them back to life. "Best let it cool down a bit," she said.

"How long do you think he's been without food, Mum?"

"Nothing of him, is there? Days I shouldn't wonder. I doubt he'll live, not now. Better your father should have drowned him along with those others – must be from the same litter."

The boy folded a towel in the bottom of the oven and then knelt to lay the kitten inside. The eyes were closed now. He was breathing slowly but this was the only sign of life.

"Shouldn't we try to feed him?" the boy said, adjusting the towel around the kitten. "Shouldn't we try something?"

"Not just yet. Warmth is what he needs first and the food comes after when he has the strength to take it."

"What will Dad say when he finds a cat in the oven?" said the boy, dreading the moment. He peered back into the depths of the oven. "He's still not moving, Mum. D'you think he'll make it?"

"Lap of the gods," said his mother. "Let him

warm up here for a few minutes and then we'll try a bottle. We'll know then right enough."

It took only a short time to wash out a bottle and teat, to water down some cow's milk; but it became obvious before they started that the teat was going to be too big for the kitten, so the boy went in frantic search of an eye dropper and found one finally upstairs on the bathroom shelf.

His mother held the kitten on her lap as she sat by the stove, and kneeling down the boy prised open the kitten's mouth and let the milk dribble in slowly. The eyes flickered and opened, and then he struggled pulling his mouth away. All the remaining strength in his feeble body seemed to be concentrated in a huge effort to keep his jaws tight shut. But some of the warm milk had dribbled through the fur and seeped into his mouth. He swallowed because he had to swallow, and he liked what he tasted. He opened his mouth for more, and the boy took his chance and squeezed the dropper. The kitten coughed and spluttered as the milk rolled down his throat, but his tongue had found the end of the dropper and discovered that this was the source. He sucked and found that the milk came through. Four droppers he sucked dry before he lay back, replete. "Back in the oven, Monty," said the boy. "I think you've had enough."

"Monty? Why Monty?" his mother asked.

"Montezuma, the Aztec king. He was a survivor, a great fighter. I read about him last term in history."

"But he was killed, wasn't he? By the Spanish. Didn't they strangle him in the end?"

"Yes," said the boy, putting the kitten in the oven. "Yes, they killed him, but it took them a long time. And we all have to die in the end, don't we, cats and kings, it doesn't make any difference. But it'll take more than a case of starvation to kill Monty off. I know this cat, Mum."

"You like him, don't you?" His mother was surprised. The boy had never shown that much affection for animals, a farmer's interest certainly but little involvement; and fourteen year old boys don't usually fall for kittens.

"He's special, Mum," the boy said. "He's not just an ordinary kitten. He'd be dead if he was, wouldn't he? What would you say if I wanted to keep him?"

His mother shook her head. "You know your Father's views. Animals stay out on the farm. We live in here, they live out there. He won't even have the dog inside the house and Sam is useful, part of the farm equipment you might say. If he won't agree to Sam, he's not likely to agree to a cat."

"But Monty deserves it," the boy pleaded.

"You tell your father that, but don't expect any help from me. I'm neutral in any arguments between you two." She put her arm around him and said warmly, "But just between you and me, I hope you win. There is something about that cat, like you say."

Mother and son were just preparing another dropper when they heard the tractor rumble into the yard outside. The whistling came nearer the door and they heard stamping boots on the step outside. The boy looked down at the open oven and there was the kitten peering out, ears pricked, eyes bright. The boy touched wood, crossed his fingers and said a quick prayer. Then the door opened.

"Finished both fields on the other side of the brook, headlands as well. But 'tis still divilish wet out there." His father sounded content and satisfied with his day, and the boy decided that this was the time to make his case.

"Dad," he said, wondering how best to begin. "Dad I found a kitten in the old granary this afternoon."

"Did you clear it out like I said?" His father bent over the sink to scrub his hands.

"Yes, Dad. It's all done."

"And the milking? Are you sure that Iris hasn't got mastitis? She felt hard enough to me last night, in the two front quarters. You sure she's all right?"

"Quite sure, Dad."

"And what about Emma? She looked as if she might calve early. Any sign?"

"No, Dad. Dad, about the kitten . . ."

"Is there a cup of tea in the pot?" His father wiped his hands and turned around to face the oven. "Gad, what the divil's that in the oven?" He stooped for a closer look, hands on his knees. "It's a perishing kitten. What the divil's a perishing kitten doing in here? Will someone tell me what the divil he's doing in that oven?"

"Dad, I've been trying to tell you. That's the kitten I found in the granary. He's been deserted by that Kitty."

"But I drowned her last lot."

"Not all of them, Dad. You must have missed this one, and I found him all starved and nearly dead. Mum and me, we've been feeding him up; and Dad, I wanted to ask you if . . ."

"Gad," said his father, and he reached in the oven and pulled the kitten out, holding him up by the scruff of the neck.

"Too old to drown now, dear," said the boy's mother. "What'll we do with him?"

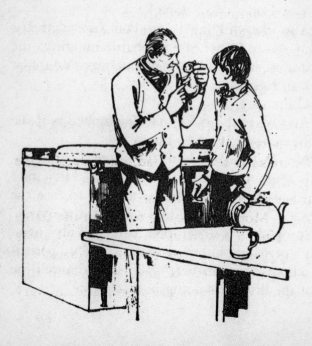

"What'll we do with him? You can't just throw him out, wouldn't be right. You'll have to keep him, won't you? Just take care you keep him out of the sitting room, that's all." He looked the kitten straight in the face, nose to nose. "Never in the sitting room, you hear me?" And he handed the kitten to the boy.

"All yours, Matthew,' he said. "What'll you call him?"

"Monty," said Matthew. "Short for Montezuma."

"Divilish silly name, but there you are, Matthew's not much better. Monty meet Matthew, Matthew meet Monty."

"D'you mean I can keep him here, Dad? He can stay?"

"Nothing else to be done, is there? Now what were you going to ask me, Matthew? You said there was something . . ."

"Nothing, Dad, it was nothing. Can't have been important. I've forgotten."

"Where's my tea then? Gad, can't a man have a cup of tea when he gets back home at night. What are you both staring at?"

And so Montezuma came to live in the farmhouse. After a few days he was moved away from the oven and into a box on the far side of the kitchen under the ironing board. But that was a long way from the stove, and he very soon found a corner of the stove by the wall where he could sleep warm and undisturbed whilst he grew slowly into adolescence.

The Third Life

It was not to be an easy transition from the farmyard to the house. Growing up, it seemed, imposed certain restrictions that Montezuma found difficult to accept. He had to learn, for instance, not to jump up on the kitchen table to lick the plates, not to yowl around the table and not to be inside when he should have been outside. Every night he was obliged to go out whatever the weather. When it was raining hard he would hide in amongst the chair legs or crawl inside the kitchen cupboard under the sink in an attempt to avoid eviction, but it did him no good. His expulsion might be postponed for a few moments but when it came it was all the more abrupt and uncomfortable. On several occasions the kitten stole away to explore the bedrooms upstairs, and once he squeezed into the pantry where all the good smells came from. But he found the rule of law was consistent and merciless. Each time he transgressed the punishment was swift and sharp; he was chased out and banished until time healed the offence and he was forgiven — again.

Gradually he was learning. He was learning all the rules and regulations, the boundaries and codes; and more and more he found it expedient to keep inside the law, ostensibly at any rate. The family all agreed that Montezuma was beginning to conform to their idea of an acceptable cat and Matthew congratulated himself upon this miraculous conversion. Even Matthew's father was beginning to admit, albeit begrudgingly, that the kitten was losing his farmyard manners. This was just the impression Montezuma wished to convey. He had merely learnt the wisdom of cunning, of guerrilla warfare as opposed to open battle. He was developing a secret weapon that would ensure the good life, and that weapon was guile. Now he would wait until the coast was quite clear before he committed his crimes. He recognised that previously his crimes of passion and greed had led to early detection and dire punishment, so now he turned to premeditated crime, meticulously planned and executed. Now he would sleep under beds and not on top of them; now he stole from the kitchen table only when the house was deserted and the door wide open for a quick escape. The efficient criminal must understand the law and then learn how best to avoid being caught. Montezuma might have continued all his life as a habitual outlaw had he not tangled that fateful afternoon with the tin of baked beans left behind on the kitchen table.

He would never even have seen the tin if the great white cockerel had not chased him away from the flower beds where he had been playing quite innocently among the snapdragons. The cockerel, a vicious Light Sussex, with a predatory beak and a flaming comb, had clearly decided that the kitten was a threat to his cackle of hens that were mining for worms in the shrubbery behind the flower-bed. He crowed noisily but the kitten paid him no attention, so he strutted purposefully towards him, wings flapping and neck feathers fluffed out. Still the kitten appeared not to notice him, and so the cockerel ran the last few feet, his neck outstretched and pecked the kitten just above his tail. Montezuma knew better than to mix it with an angry cockerel, so he beat a retreat, hissing and spitting back at the cockerel from a safe distance. By the back door he turned again to arch his back in a final gesture of indignation, but the cockerel had forgotten him and was feeding with his hens in the flower-bed. It was then that Montezuma spied the green tin standing like

a beckoning beacon on the kitchen table. Tins, he knew from delving into dustbins, were always worth further investigation. Everyone was out of the house, that much he was sure of; because he had watched all three of them setting off down the farm track towards the sheep fields. They were gone and someone had left the door wide open. It was an invitation not to be refused. With a final look around he stole into the kitchen, jumped onto the chair by the stove and then from the chair onto the table. He was alone with the green tin and one look told him that the tin was far from empty.

Montezuma licked the sides clean first before pushing his head further in so that he could eat his way down towards the bottom of the tin. It was a delectable feast and he did not hurry it.

Several times he came up for air to lick his whiskers and to listen out for footsteps, before plunging his head in once again. There was one layer of beans covered in sauce on the bottom that he still could not reach, just a few, but Montezuma had to have them. Determined not to waste anything he forced his head down, until the tin felt tight around his neck; then he wrapped his tongue around the last of the beans and licked the tin clean. He was searching in every corner now for the last traces of the tomato sauce and was licking around for the last time in case he had left any behind. Satisfied, yet disappointed that the baked bean orgy was over, Montezuma called it a day and pulled his head out. It might be better to say that he tried to pull his head out, because try as he might his head would not be pulled free. Each time he tried to jerk his head away the tin stayed with it. He used his front paws in an attempt to anchor the tin on the table, but he could not grip sufficiently for the tin to hold as he pulled his head once again in an attempt to break free.

Panic was setting in by now. Each attempt that failed only increased his terror. It was becoming hot inside the tin and he found the air more and more difficult to breathe. There didn't seem to be enough of it, and he sensed that time was running out. He whipped over onto his back and with his front paws tried to prise the tin off his head. He twisted this way and that in a frantic effort scrabbling at the rim of the tin with his claws; but the tin was stuck fast. Within a few minutes he had lost the notion of his position on the table, and stepped out into mid-air falling heavily on the corner of the chair before hitting the floor. He landed badly on his side and when he finally found his feet again he was totally disorientated. Like a blind man he staggered around the kitchen into cupboards and chair legs, tripping over bowls and brooms until he fell down the back doorstep and found himself in the cobbled yard outside.

Montezuma came out into the sun by the water tank, the tin can riveted over his face. He called out in his fear as loudly as he could and this attracted the attention of the white cockerel and his hens. With an hysterical squawking they scattered in all directions leaving Montezuma alone on the cobbles wandering in aimless circles and yowling pitifully. Every few moments he stopped and tried again to loosen the tin, but he had tried every way he could think of and it was all to no avail. He was weakening all the time, and each effort to free himself was more feeble than the one before.

Matthew and his parents had left the house in a hurry to pick out one of the ewes that looked unwell. Matthew had thought it might be Black Udder and it needed the three of them to catch her to be sure. He had been proved right and they had treated the ewe before returning home. As they came into the yard all three saw the kitten at the same time walking drunkenly towards them like some feline Ned Kelly. Matthew reached him first and held him fast while his father pulled on the tin.

"Mind his neck," Matthew shouted. "You'll break his neck."

"He'll suffocate if he stays like this," his father said. "Suffocated, broken neck, it's all the same. You hold him tight. Mum, you run and fetch some of that liquid soap. Might help to loosen it."

Montezuma was only semi-conscious now and so fought instinctively against the hands that held him. His eyes felt as if they would burst in his head and he was totally consumed by his terror.

"Easy, Monty," said Matthew, releasing a hand to stroke the kitten. "Easy, you'll be all right. We'll have it off in no time. You'll see." The kitten relaxed, momentarily calmed, only to start up again slashing his claws wildly with renewed viciousness.

The soap arrived and within seconds Matthew's mother had dribbled in enough so that the tin could be turned. Matthew clutched the kitten firmly gathering all the legs securely together, while his father tried now to unscrew the tin from the head. This time it came away easily in his hand.

For just a second Montezuma remained still in Matthew's hands, his eyes screwed up against the light, taking the fresh air deep into his lungs. Then he dug his claws in and sprang free. He ran as he had never run, going nowhere in particular, just away. He sprinted under the iron gate that led to the farmyard, squeezed through the sheep netting and out into the meadow beyond. There the trunk of the old beech tree loomed up in front of him and he climbed it because it was there and because to go up was to get away. He climbed until he could climb no longer, until he ran out of tree.

Matthew followed and came through into the farmyard only just in time to catch sight of the kitten scaling the sheer straight trunk of the tree. He watched, shielding his eyes against the sun as Montezuma crawled out onto an upper branch and finally came to rest some thirty feet above the duck pond.

"Where the divil's he gone now?" said his father, still holding the baked bean tin in his hand.

"He's up there," said Matthew. "Frightened half to death."

"Matthew," his mother said, "I haven't used baked beans in weeks. Have you been at my tins again?"

"I was hungry," Matthew admitted. "I just had a few, that's all."

"Gad, you're a baked bean fanatic," said his father. "And you've been told often enough about tidying up after yourself. It's your fault, my lad. Could have killed that kitten you know."

"Didn't know you cared," said Matthew.

"Don't you start, you two," said Matthew's mother. "There's poor Monty stuck up that tree, so don't start. We've got to get him down, he won't come down on his own — not from that height."

"I'll go up after him," said Matthew.

"You can't go all the way up there," his mother said. "What happens if you fall?"

"He won't fall," said Matthew's father. "He'll be all right. He's spent most of his life climbing trees, climbs like a monkey – he'll be all right."

Matthew felt less confident as he began the climb. The bark was slippery from the previous day's rain and the higher he climbed the more the wind seemed to gust. He climbed carefully, securing good footholds and testing each branch before he put his full weight onto it. He had climbed the old beech often enough before but always for fun. This was serious and he was not enjoying it. He had lost sight of Monty now and was concentrating on the climb. From below his father kept shouting up detailed instructions about how he would do it if he were up there, about grip and balance; and his mother kept up a chorus of: "Oh be careful, dear. Do be careful."

He found Montezuma crouching at the end of a long tapering branch that hung out over the pond. The branch looked thick enough and safe enough near the trunk, but the further away it stretched the more fragile it looked. Matthew stood in the fork of the tree and considered all the alternatives, trying to ignore the warnings and advice from below. He could not climb out along the branch to Monty — the branch would not take his weight. He needed a net to throw out over the cat, but there was no-one who could bring a net up to him — neither his father nor his mother could climb trees — at least he had never seen them. He would have to talk the kitten back to safety, that was the only way.

"Monty," he said in as soothing a tone as he could manage. "It's me, Monty. You can't stay out there all day. You'll be all right now. I'll take you down. Come on then, come on. I won't hurt you."

But the kitten crouched low, glued to the branch like lichen. He blinked back at Matthew, swallowing hard and mewing weakly every so often. Matthew talked on in a consoling, sympathetic tone; but he received no encouragement from Montezuma who never moved a muscle.

From down below his father was shouting up to him. "Can't you get him down?" A question which Matthew didn't feel he could answer politely.

"Fire Brigade," his mother shouted up. "What about the Fire Brigade?" They looked so small down there in the yard. Matthew felt his parents had been getting smaller in recent years, but he had never seen them this small.

"Not yet," Matthew shouted back. "Not yet. I'll try one more thing."

"Do be careful, dear. Do be careful." His mother's voice sounded hysterical, but then it always did whenever she shouted.

Matthew held onto the branch above him, and edged out onto Montezuma's branch stepping sideways like a cautious crab. The two branches ran parallel for a few yards and then the upper one that Matthew was holding onto came to an abrupt halt. Matthew went as far as he could and then released the upper branch. For a moment he stood balancing with nothing to hold onto. The branch swayed underneath him and he lowered himself carefully until he was sitting astride the branch his hands clasping it firmly in front of him. Like this he pulled himself along inch by inch until he knew he could go no further. The kitten was still well out of reach.

"That's far enough." His father's shout was sharp. "No further. That's far enough. The branch won't take the weight. No further."

Matthew knew he was right, but he was nearly there and it was only a few more feet. He lay now flat along the branch gripping behind with his feet, his hands holding on in front of him. "Come on Monty, come on down. Please, there's a good kitten. Come on now." But as he released one hand to reach out towards the cat, he lost his balance and had to grab at the branch suddenly to retrieve himself. Alarmed, the kitten backed away, lost his grip and tumbled down through the air towards the pond. Matthew watched for the splash and saw his father running down across the yard towards the pond. The ducks evacuated the pond noisily, leaving Matthew's father alone in the pond striding waist deep to the spot where Montezuma had fallen in. Matthew waited, closed his eyes and prayed. When he opened them his father was shouting

up at him and laughing, holding up a dripping kitten. "Got him. He's all right. The little divil's still breathing."

By the time Matthew had made the descent, his father was out of the pond and had pulled off his shoes. He was sitting on the ground taking his socks off and wringing out the water.

"Your father will catch his death," said Matthew's mother, who was holding on to Montezuma in a vice-like grip. "Here's your Monty," she said. "You take him. And for God's sake hang on to him. You worry me to death, you two. First you go climbing up trees and then he goes jumping into cold ponds — at his age. You should know better. Could have killed you both and all for what? For a kitten."

"For Monty," said Matthew, rubbing the kitten dry with the tail of his shirt. "This is no ordinary cat, you know. Can you imagine my Dad jumping into a pond to rescue any other cat? He's dropped plenty of kittens into this pond, but this is the first one he's ever pulled out and that's a fact."

"And the last," said his father wriggling his wet toes. "Definitely the last."

Montezuma's career as a sneak thief was at an end — for the time being anyway. Certainly, half empty tin cans held no fascination for him. Of course there were other temptations, but he was off baked beans for life.

The Fourth Life

Montezuma spent the first summer and winter of his young life exploring his territory. During these months he awoke to his own potential as a hunter. The days were slept away peacefully by the kitchen stove; but at dusk, well fed and rested, he would slip out silently through the back door and be gone for the night.

Matthew saw little of him during this time. He might spot him skulking around the hedge-rows on his way down the road to milking in the morning, or find him curled up in the barn when he went to fetch the hay. He loved to watch Montezuma basking in the summer sun, or chasing leaves in autumn, or stalking stealthily through the long grass in the orchard. But Matthew never played with him. For him, Montezuma was no plaything, just a companion that he liked to be with. He felt no proprietary rights over the cat. It was not his cat; he was Montezuma and that was enough.

Montezuma felt at ease in his home – most of the time. When Matthew and his mother were in the house he could sleep secure by his stove. For food he went to either of them, or both if he could get away with it, and always felt assured of a friendly response. He liked to sit on Matthew's knee and sharpen his claws on the shoulder of his jacket, rubbing up against his ear. But the sound of the father's footsteps was like an air-raid siren to him. If asleep he would awake, look frantically around and dash into the deepest, darkest corner he could find, and then flee the room as soon as he could. Matthew's father had never been deliberately cruel, not as such. But a cat knows when he is not welcome. Countless times Montezuma had been tipped out of his chair and chased out of the kitchen. It was true that Matthew's father had flung a boot in his direction once or twice when he had been yowling for his food, but he had never hit him. Now they simply avoided each other and had come to terms with that arrangement. They could live together if they lived apart.

Montezuma had grown into a huge, stripey ginger tom with a long tail that he carried proud and high, unless he was hunting. His ears were pointed sharply and were long enough to be

those of a wild cat. The farmyard was his kingdom; he had made it so. There were other cats
that occasionally strayed onto his land, but he
made sure they didn't stay for long. Each
intruder found to his cost that Montezuma stood
his ground.

He was fast becoming a lethal hunter, with
a preference for ambush. His favourite killing
ground was in the hedgerows and ditches in the
long barley field that ran along the lane down to
the river. It was here he had served his hunting
apprenticeship, discovered by trial and error the
techniques that worked, and the habits of his
prey. He knew every little track and hole; he
learned to use the noise of the wind as camou-
flage and to lie in ambush as still as a log. He
had come to gauge the speed of their reaction
to his attack, to recognise and appreciate their
individual capacity for retaliation and survival.

It was only with Sam, the farm's sheep and
cattle dog, that Montezuma felt unsure of himself. Sam was never allowed in the house, so that
the problem only arose outside the farm. Here,
out in the open, they eyed each other at a distance and went their separate ways harbouring
feelings of mutual suspicion and fear. Sam
understood that this cat had come to stay by
the frequency of their meetings and Montezuma
knew that the dog belonged to the farm and was

no direct threat to his feline supremacy of the farmyard.

Sam was a bushy black and white collie with long white teeth and a mouth that seemed to pant perpetually. He had that perception and intuitive intelligence that a good sheepdog should possess, and he sensed that it might be wise to give the young cat elbow room, for the moment anyway.

The two co-existed as only animals can with a degree of tolerance inspired by self-interest. But self-interest in two such close neighbours must inevitably clash, and so it did one Sunday afternoon on the front lawn outside the farmhouse.

As usual the bone from the Sunday joint of lamb had been handed to Sam, whose appetite for bones, or for anything else for that matter, was inexhaustible. Now Sam did not usually eat his bone at once – few bones were worth eating until they had lain in the earth for some weeks. His usual procedure was to trot down the lane to Mr. Varley's vegetable garden, the softest bed of earth in the parish. There he would bury the bone busily, looking furtively over his shoulder all the while; and when he had nudged all the earth back over with his nose, he would return to the farm with an air of achievement, his nose caked a rich red-brown. For an intelligent dog this was a foolish thing to do. Everyone knew where he buried his bones, Mr. Varley best of all, who dug up the bones whenever he discovered them and that was often enough. However, this particular afternoon Sam was tired, and it was hot, and the bone was big; so he lay down on the front lawn and gnawed contentedly in the sunshine.

Now Montezuma had always entertained hopes of the Sunday bone, and from his vantage point by the stove he watched Matthew leave the table and carry the great bone outside. He followed only on the off chance, and watched from the shrubbery as Matthew made the dog sit and take the bone gently in his mouth. The dog waited for Matthew to go back inside, standing possessively over his bone; and then he turned and padded onto the lawn, droped his bone and lay down neatly, relishing the feast to come. Montezuma emerged cautiously from the shadows of the fuschia, and sat down on the path a safe distance away. He had a tick in his ear and it needed scratching. The dog turned at the movement and growled a warning. He picked up his bone and moved away towards the garden wall.

This wall was a favourite place for Montezuma. It was flat on the top and could be used either for basking in the sun or as one of the

best observation posts for local hunting. He had caught a wagtail from there only the week before. He retreated from the shrubbery and in a flanking movement ran round the other side of the wall and sprang up easily.

Sam was busily involved and unable at first to decide which end of the bone to begin. After much consideration he decided finally to stand up and strip it wherever the meat was most plentiful. He planted one paw firmly on it and began his meal. From above him on the wall the cat watched biding his time.

The phone rang back in the kitchen and

Matthew's mother answered it as she always did. No one else ever moved when the phone rang. "Yes," she said, "Oh, we are sorry about that." And then, "I can't think how it can have happened. I'm, so sorry." Matthew and his father stopped eating their apple pie and listened. "Through onto the garden. Oh deary me, deary me, it must be a terrible mess. Yes, yes. Well, we'll be right down. One of us'll be right down." She put the phone down and ran back into the kitchen. "It's your cows, Matthew; they're out in Mr. Varley's garden, his vegetable garden. You'd best get down there. Hurry now."

"Take Sam," said his father. "And tell Mr. Varley I'll be right down to help. Go on lad, get going else there won't be any garden left." But Matthew was already gone, calling for Sam as he ran down the garden path.

Sam was reluctant to leave his bone. He had barely started his feast and he wouldn't leave his treasure out on the lawn exposed and vulnerable. "Come on, Sam. Leave it!" Matthew shouted at him and whistled him up. Sam compromised, picked up the bone and ran over towards him. "Not the bone, Sam, you blockhead. It's you I want. Drop it, drop it now." Sam obeyed, as he always did in the end, and dropped the bone in under the fuschia hedge, out of sight. He backed out, cast an eye around to make sure that no-one had seen him and then sprinted away up the lane after Matthew, who was still whistling for him. Montezuma had watched it all from the top of his wall. He waited until boy and dog were out of sight and then he moved in, bounding across the lawn and into the fuschia hedge. The bone was too heavy to move and anyway this was a perfect place to settle down. Montezuma crouched down on all fours and set to, still alert however to the possibility of surprise. His joy was unbounded as he found more and more layers of rich succulent red meat. He ate on, oblivious now to the world outside the shadows of the hedge. He had quite forgotten the dog and it never occurred to him that it might return to retrieve its bone.

Matthew and Sam were away for some time. It was not difficult to drive the cows back through the broken gate and out into the meadow again, but the explanations and condolences could not be hurried. Mr. Varley had been a neighbour as long as Matthew had been alive and in all that time Matthew could not remember hearing a harsh word from him. And even now as the old man gazed out over his ruined vegetable garden, he simply shook his head sadly and puffed his pipe. He blamed no-one. "S'pose it'll save me rotovating it." he said. "We've had a wonderful lot of vegetables this year, so I can't grumble."

Matthew tried to apologise and mentioned insurance money, but Mr. Varley would have none of it. "Not your fault," he said. "Not anyone's fault. The cows broke through the gate. It's no use blaming them, is it now? And insurance you say. No, I'll not have any of that kind of thing. These things happen and there's nothing the insurance can do except pay me money; and it doesn't take money to dig over a vegetable patch, does it? You go home my lad, and tell your Dad not to worry. We'll put it all to rights, you'll see."

Sam waited impatiently as the apologies dragged on. He had done his work and now he wanted to get back to his bone. When Matthew had finished apologising for the umpteenth time he turned to go. Sam could wait no longer. At the bottom of the lane he left his master and ran on ahead, his mouth already watering in anticipation.

By the time Montezuma heard the dog, it was too late. He was caught unawares and was panicked into a hasty flight. He shot out of the back of the fuschia hedge as the dog came in the front, but the dog had seen him on his bone and that was enough. The truce was broken and it was war.

Behind the fuschia hedge was the piggery and the door was open as it always is in the summer to let the air in. Montezuma saw it as a way out. The pen doors at the back of the pig pens would be open and he could make his escape into the orchard and up a tree. But it was dark inside, darker than usual. He looked both ways but there was no time for a considered decision: the dog was close behind. Montezuma leapt the wall into the pen at the end of the piggery and landed in the muck at the other side. Then, and only then, did he realise that the pen doors were shut fast and that he was trapped. He whipped round

and tried to leap the wall of the pen again. From there he might make it to the safety of the rafters. But the dog was already on the wall and looking down at him, his teeth gleaming white and his hackles up. The dog did not hesitate and Montezuma was hurled to the ground. He could feel the hot breath on his eyes and squirmed away from the teeth, rolling onto his back and slashing out at the face that bore down on him. He felt teeth sink into his leg, but took heart when he heard the dog yelp in pain as his claws flashed across the dog's nose drawing blood. Montezuma's ears were laid flat against his head, and he knew now that this was a fight to the death. Even if he could run, there was nowhere to run to. He had to fight it out. He set up a hideous yowling and spat viciously, swiping accurately at the dog's eyes as he came into the attack.

Sam was going for the throat. He had lost all traces of domesticity. He was back to the wolf. His teeth were bared, his face transformed from the soft, loving sheepdog to the ruthless killer. He had made two hits near the cat's throat conceding a scratched eye and nose, but his blood was up and no cat scratch could deter him now. He leapt forward again onto the cat and struck downwards, his teeth closing over the cat's ear. He had him now and shook him until he could hold the grip no longer.

Matthew heard the rumpus from half-way down the lane and he could guess what had happened. By the time he arrived there was no stopping Sam, who was quite beyond reason. He leant over the wall and tried to pull him off, but the dog turned on him like a cobra, snapping at his wrist. Matthew ran for the bucket of water he used for mixing the barley for the pigs. He filled it quickly from the tap and ran back, throwing it over Sam. Then he vaulted in over the rails, opened the pen doors to the outside and bundled Sam out whilst he was still shaking the water from his face.

Montezuma lay on his back, his front paws still instinctively sweeping the air above, blinded by the blood from his ear. Matthew talking to him, stroking his side to calm him. "All over, Monty," he said. "You're all right. You'll be all right." He picked him up carefully. "What did you do to get Sam all riled up like that? I've seen him kill a rat once, but he was never that angry. What did you do?"

Back in the kitchen they cleaned Montezuma up. The wounds were superficial, although his ear was badly torn and his leg would need stitching. Once the blood was cleared away, he looked more his old self. They took him to the vet who stitched him up and injected him; and for two or three days after he lay by his stove not eating and going out only when he had to. "He's sulking," said Matthew's mother.

"He's had his come-uppance," said Matthew's father. "That Sam taught him a thing or two."

"He's in pain," Matthew said. "You can tell, he must be in terrible pain."

But they all three had it wrong. Montezuma's pride had been hurt to the quick. He had made an elementary mistake in allowing himself to be taken by surprise. He felt no enmity towards the dog, but was consumed by a grim determination never to be caught off guard again.

The ear never straightened out after that, and his leg mended slowly. Within a week or so Montezuma was back on patrol, his pride damaged but intact. For his part, Sam had a gash across his face, a scratched eye and torn nose; it was enough to persuade him to avoid another confrontation. The two eyed each other with mutual respect now, acknowledging each other as the king in his own world.

The Fifth Life

Matthew had left school and had come back to work full time on the farm alongside his father. Like Montezuma, Matthew was fully fledged now and the two came to spend more and more time together. Farming is a solitary way of life and Matthew welcomed the company of the cat as he followed him to all corners of the farm. He never called Montezuma to come, but he expected him to be there with him and he always was. No matter where he was or what he was doing, sheep-shearing, hedge-laying, hay-making or out shooting, the cat would be there even if Matthew could not see him.

By the third winter of his life Montezuma had inveigled his way into the inner sanctum and established himself in the sitting room. It had been a gradual, imperceptible invasion, but he had now come to occupy the arm of the sofa nearest to the fire. Matthew's father had put up a stern resistance, bowling him out through the door and back into the kitchen on several occasions. "I'll not have it," he'd say. "I spend all my days with beasts and I'll not have the mucky things taking over in here." But Montezuma was immune to his insults and crept back in surreptitiously, hiding behind the sofa. One evening, however when Matthew's father was too tired to bother, Montezuma was allowed to clamber up onto the sofa and stay there, and from that moment the cat knew the battle was won. Matthew and his mother were tactful enough never to draw attention to the cat as he purred provocatively on his perch overlooking the fire. The exchanged knowing looks and smiled secretly at the subtlety of Montezuma's quiet victory.

It was in the middle of lambing, sometime after Christmas, that the unbelievable happened. Matthew came in after evening milking. He had checked the in-lamb ewes out in the fields, bringing in those that looked nearest to lambing into the safety of the big barn. He called out from the back door as he came in: "Could be snow on the way, so I brought the ewes inside again." But his mother was waving at him to be quiet, her finger pressed against her lips. On tiptoe they approached the door of the sitting room and peeped in. Matthew's father lay back on the sofa, his feet occupying Montezuma's sleeping patch. Montezuma however had chosen the only soft place still available to him on the sofa. He lay stretched out on the old man's stomach, gently rising and falling in rhythm with the snoring. But Montezuma was not asleep; he was too content to sleep. He looked up towards the door and winked at them, the smile of a sybarite unashamedly on his face. The two behind the door were convulsed with mirth. They were quite unable to control their delight and clung to each other in an effort to stifle their laughter, but it was too late. Like the fee-fi-fo-fum giant, Matthew's father awoke at their muffled giggling and the cat was astute enough to leap for cover, but it did not move fast enough. He was picked up roughly by the nape of his neck and held up by his adversary whom he now faced nose to nose, his feet dangling in the air. "Never again," said Matthew's father. "No cat climbs on me and lives, not twice. Never again." And he threw the cat out through the door, past Matthew and his mother who were still laughing too much to lift a finger in protest. Montezuma picked himself out from under the pump in the kitchen and ran out into the night, bruised but not bowed. He would be back to claim his rights.

It was a cold, still night and the cat had been

inside for most of the day. At the end of the garden path he stopped, lifted his nose and sniffed the air. There was a strange heaviness he had not experienced before and it alarmed him. He heard the dogs barking at each other across the valley as they did every night, but then sharper to his ears the call of the distant she-cat. Montezuma listened intently for a moment, plotted the direction of the call and calculated his course. Then he padded away under the gate, up through the hedgerow and down across the black fields towards the river.

That night the snows came, gently at first in huge floating flakes, the kind of snow that builds up quickly and silently. By breakfast the next morning the snow was a foot high around the house and the world had turned perfect outside. The roads had merged into hedges and the hedges into the flat fields. The mud by the gateways was covered under the same universal white shroud. The farm was new again and deathly quiet.

Matthew was not worried about his sheep; it was far better to have most of the flock out in the cold fresh air even in snow, than cooped up in the barns where disease could spread quickly. He had already checked the ewes brought in the night before and helped to deliver twin lambs before he came back in for his breakfast. It was then that he realised that Montezuma was still not back.

"Seen Monty?" he said. "He usually comes over and checks the sheep with me, but I've not seen him about. Have you?"

"He'll be back," said his father. "He always comes back, that cat does. Night out on the tiles I shouldn't wonder. Little divil."

"Sit down, Matthew and eat your breakfast," said his mother. "And stop worrying about that cat. It's the sheep you should worry about. If this snow goes on . . ."

"It won't, Mum. It's stopped already and the sun's working on it now. Won't be anything left by the evening."

"You watch those sheep, my lad. They can only stand so much depth of snow. Better to be safe than sorry."

"Don't worry, Dad," Matthew said, "I've seen them. They're all right. They found cover in under the trees by the brook."

"You counted them?" his father went on. "You're sure they're all there?"

"Every one, Dad. They're all there." But Matthew had his mind elsewhere. Montezuma had always been back by the morning. He would hear him yowling on the window ledge outside his bedroom window; he would talk to him as the cat followed him around on his early morning work. He had never gone missing before.

It was almost all sheep work those deep winter days. His father had taken the milking in hand and left the flock to him. It was an incessant round of checking the in-lamb ewes, the single couples and the double couples and feeding them; injecting the new-born lambs, ringing the tails, feeding the tame lambs and then back to help with another lambing. So far it had been a good lambing year with no scour and very few stillborn lambs. There had been problems with one set of twin lambs getting tied up with each other inside and presenting themselves backwards, but they had only lost two living lambs and one ewe that never recovered after giving birth.

So Matthew was busy all that day, too busy to do anything about Montezuma. From time to time he thought of the cat and called out for him, but there was no answering cry. There was no time to go looking for him.

The snow did thaw during the afternoon but Matthew was sure it would be gone by the next day. That was why he left most of the flock outside that night, bringing in again only those about to lamb and those freshly lambed. Last thing before he turned in, he went over to check the sheep; as he came back across the yard, scuffling through the muddy snow, he called out once more for the cat and listened for the response, but none came. It was just as he reached the top of the granary steps that he thought he heard Montezuma, a faint call, possibly coming from the sheep field across the brook. Matthew ran down towards the brook and then stood silent in the snow to listen again. He called out time and again but heard nothing more. The wind was getting up and he was cold. The cat would come back when he was ready, he thought; but he went to bed that night troubled and unconvinced by his own artificial optimism.

While they slept the blizzard struck. The snow swirled around the house, whipped up from the fields around and driven by hurricane-force winds that battered the house. Matthew was woken up by the rattle of his windows and a door banging outside in the farmyard. He sat up in bed to listen to the howl of the storm. It seemed to him that the house might be uprooted at any moment and carried off; as the gusts hit the house he felt it shake and shiver in its foundations. He knew he would have to get up; the sheep should not be outside in this. He met his father, who had woken with the same thought, in the passage outside. Both dressed quickly, pulling on heavy overcoats and buttoning up against the storm.

Matthew fetched Sam from the shippen where he slept and they stumbled out together across the meadow and down the hill towards the brook. They took shelter in the spinney under the old quarry before crossing the bridge into the sheep field. At times they had to walk backwards to prevent the snow stinging their eyes. Each had to pull the other out of great drifts that had gathered like breaking waves across the field. Every word had to be screamed out against the wind, and even so in the end they had to resort to sign language. The torches they were carrying proved useless, unable to penetrate the driving snow. They could feel their cheeks freezing up. The snow stung their eyes, blinding them. They fought it, bending into the wind forcing their legs forward.

Finally they discovered the sheep sheltering down in the corner of the field where the hedge joined the brook. They were packed together, a great off-white huddle in the snow. Sam worked well that night. Bounding through drifts of snow several times his own height he drove them cleanly across the bridge, up over the hill and into the shelter of the yard. It was a slow drive, the sheep wanting to return to the shelter they had left.

Counting was difficult. The sheep moved incessantly around each other like massed molecules. After two counts the grim truth had to be accepted – they were missing six ewes with their lambs. A further trek out into the fields proved fruitless and the storm drove them back indoors, exhausted and cold. In the comforting warmth of the kitchen Matthew and his father cradled the hot tea that was pressed into their hands. They sat in silence around the stove, each buried in his own despondency. "Monty will have a job getting back in this," said Matthew.

"Never you worry," his mother said. "He'll be hiding up somewhere, like the sheep."

"I hope you're right, my dear," Matthew's father sounded broken and old. "Soon as the storm blows itself out, we'll have to search every drift. But if it goes on like this they won't last long; nothing will, not in this."

For two days and nights the blizzard continued. Water pipes froze, the electricity was cut off and then the telephone went dead. They were besieged on all sides by drifts of snow that seemed to have grown every time they looked, cutting off the light from the windows and covering the lanes from one hedge top to the other. Tractors were useless. Every bale of hay had to be manhandled over the snow. It was all they could do to keep the stock fed and watered,

and then every spare moment was spent shovelling the snow away from the doorways and paths in an effort to keep open the lifelines to the barns.

On the morning of the third day, the wind dropped and the sun shone. They could begin the search for the missing animals. Montezuma was nowhere to be found. Matthew had searched every barn and shippen he could reach. He called out across the white wasteland, but even as he called he knew there could be no hope. With the snow more than three feet thick everywhere and drifts of twenty feet, even his faith in the cat's ability to survive had faded. He turned his mind to the missing ewes and tried to forget the cat.

Every available hour of daylight now was spent probing in the drifts for the sheep. The washing line pole, broom handles, anything that was long enough was brought into service. They worked systematically around the perimeter drifts of each sheep field. On that first day after the storm they searched the drifts in the field by the brook and found nothing. But the next morning they discovered their first missing ewe trapped in a drift up against the spinney. She was lying dead with her lamb beside her. It was an ill omen, but just finding her gave the rescuers the encouragement they needed to work on. Like his father, Matthew was consumed by an exhaustion so profound that they had ceased to talk to one another. Once fed and warmed up back at the house, they were out again probing into drifts in a tacitly agreed determination not to give up.

Three days later, a week after the storm began, when hope of finding anything alive had all but vanished, Matthew felt his stick strike something soft. Like a desperate angler who cannot believe the pull on the end of his line, Matthew refused to believe his first impression. He probed once more close to the same hole, gently. His stick met a little resistance at first and then sank into something that moved as he touched it. He screamed his excitement and in a few seconds his mother and father were at his side probing to confirm his find. The sticks were thrown to one side and the digging began. It was a huge drift that had climbed half way up the trunk of a great oak tree whose roots bulged out from the bank creating a warren of holes and hiding places, a favourite playing place for the lambs. In half an hour they had broken through into the roof of the hollow. Matthew pulled the snow away feverishly and peered through. "They're here," he said. "They're all here, all five, and the lambs as well, and everyone's alive!" As if to prove the point one of the lambs set up a tremendous bleating. The rest was easy, they scraped away the side of the hole, reached in and hauled the sheep out one by one onto the snow.

Matthew was reaching in to catch the last lamb that didn't seem to want to leave his sanctuary, when he noticed there was something lying in a hole behind one of the roots. At first he thought it was another lamb for it was covered with a thin coating of snow, but lambs do not mew and they are not ginger striped underneath. Montezuma was staggering towards him, shaking the snow from his back. He looked up at Matthew, his eyes squinting against the sun. Matthew reached in and picked him up carefully. He turned to his mother and father. "Look what I've found," he said. "Back from the dead!"

The Sixth Life

For Matthew it was neither daffodils nor primroses that heralded the spring, it was the call of the invisible wood pigeons from the high branches of the elms behind the old cob barn. He stopped to listen one morning as they answered each other across the yard. Spring itself had been a hard time on the farm with the lambing barely over and the problems of tilling the barley weighing more heavily each day. The long dry days were spent on the tractors, ploughing, harrowing and tilling; and when it was wet there was the frustration and worry that it might never stop and the barley might never be tilled. The cooing of the pigeons brought Matthew the hope of summer and the memory of the sun warm on his back.

Montezuma was with him as usual that morning, but he was keeping his distance for they were driving yearlings out to grass, and Sam was running about looking busy and officious. Like Matthew, Montezuma had heard the pigeons for the first time and welcomed the sound, but for different reasons. He pricked his good ear and lifted his head, but the sunlight through the filigree branches dazzled him and he had to turn away. But he had registered the place, and he would remember.

Montezuma was now in his hunting prime and this was the beginning of the hunting season, for birds that is. The secret of his success was his acute computer memory. Every nest was surveyed and recorded meticulously. For the next month or so he charted the comings and goings of the parent birds as they fed their young. Sitting silent and immobile in the shadow of the hedges, the cat kept his vigil from the early strident cheepings from the nest to the appearance of the fledglings. He was always there to pick up the rejects or those unfortunate enough to fall from the nest before they could fly. Any robin suicidal enough to sit on a nest within reach of the ground was plucked off and eaten.

No one much liked Montezuma during the bird-hunting season. Boots were thrown more often than usual and there was never any reward nor even congratulations when he brought in a murdered pied wagtail and dropped it on the kitchen floor for all to admire. But his talent was not appreciated and so he came home less often, preferring to spend his days patrolling his killing ground around the farm. And all the time he kept the cooing pigeons under constant observation.

The ploughing was all done now, the winter mud replaced by dust. The mowing grass was three feet high on the front meadow; they would be hay harvesting any day now. The air was humming with summer.

The cat stood under the eaves of the old barn and listened. Several times every day he came back to check on his pigeons. On several occasions he had tried to ambush the parents while they were out foraging, but with no success. Montezuma knew his chances were slim, but he welcomed the challenge. A pigeon was a rare prize and an awkward quarry, worth the waiting. Any day now the young would be teetering on the edge of the nest in the old cob wall and taking their first tentative steps in experimental flight. This was the moment he had waited for. Pigeons are best caught either when they are very old or very young either too old to move or too young to know.

The nest above him was strangely quiet this afternoon, and to begin with the cat supposed the parent bird was in there with them, but from

the beech tree by the pond he heard the cooing
and spotted the pair of them just as they clapped
their wings and flew up out of the tree to the
top of the barn. The nest must be empty. Montezuma ran across the cobbles and shinned up a
dead elm that overlooked the barn. He surprised
a squirrel climbing on the blind side of the tree
but did not give chase: he was no random
hunter. From an overhanging branch he could
better observe the nest, but he did not need to
investigate further. Above him, along the ridge
of the lichen covered roof, he saw the entire
family – three fledglings and their parents lined

up alongside each other. It was a huge leap from the branch to the slate roof, but Montezuma had done it many times before. He walked out carefully as far as the branch would support him and then launched himself into the air twenty feet above the ground. His landing was perfect, his claws sinking into the grey lichen to give him purchase as he scrambled up the slates over and onto the ridge. The parent birds had flown already but at the other end of the roof the three grey fledglings seemed unable or unwilling to fly. As the cat approached they jostled into each other, turning this way and that in alarm. Then one of them took the plunge and fluttered off the ridge, half falling, half flying down the roof beating its wings in a frantic effort to achieve air power; this it finally did and soared away downwards into the yard below to land on the water trough. There were just the two left now for the cat, but that was enough for him. He inched his way along the ridge towards them, his tail whisking from side to side in anticipation. A few feet away he stopped, crouched and eyed them hypnotically. All his power was concentrated in the back legs, his paws shifting to find a perfect balance, the perfect starting block on the narrow ridge. The two young pigeons never moved until they saw the cat leap; then they were gone in a flurry of flapping, impotent wings. But the nearest one had left it too late and fell to the ground in the yard, the upper feathers of the wings torn away.

Montezuma was disappointed – it had not been a clean kill; he had misjudged their speed. But down there below him in the yard lay his quarry struggling feebly to lift itself from the ground. That was compensation enough. The other two had gone and the parent birds with them, but that did not matter any more. Montezuma was in no hurry to find his way down across the roof to the top of the yard wall; the bird was crippled and the cat was sure of his prey.

He came in through the yard gate by the dung heap and froze. The pigeon was lying where he had expected, its wings still flapping, feebly now. But Montezuma was not looking at the pigeon. From out of the darkness of the shippen at the far end of the yard came a huge black tomcat, shining and sleek in the sun. He had seen the pigeon and was about to move in for the kill. The two cats saw each other almost at the same moment and had stopped dead in their tracks. All that moved in the yard was the dying pigeon.

Montezuma set up his battle cry and manoeuvred closer, his back arched and bristling. The pigeon was forgotten. His challenge was hurled back at him across the yard and the two cats crept slowly towards each other uttering dire warnings, none of which were heeded. This was a cat Montezuma had not met before and he would take his time before he attacked. He watched the black cat move and noted the strength in his shoulders: he glared into its yellow eyes and probed for weakness there but found none. Once again he arched his back and hissed out his defiance. But the black cat blinked, crouched, and sprang. The two cats met in midair and fell to the ground, rolling together in a bundle down the slope towards the drain. Montezuma regained his feet first and struck out across the black cat's nose. But the black cat was young and knew only how to attack. He sprang forward again but this time Montezuma was prepared and swayed to one side, catching the cat a glancing blow on his head as he passed. Blood trickled down through the black fur and dropped onto the yard.

In most fights this would have been enough to finish it and Montezuma stood his ground now waiting for the black cat to retreat and call it a day. To encourage him he began the baying cry of victory. For several minutes the black cat sat down at a safe distance from Montezuma, seeming disinterested in continuing the combat; but none the less he would not give way, he

would not concede. He was on Montezuma's territory and yet he would not give way. Once again Montezuma's victory call resounded around the barns; but the black cat sat and watched him, unimpressed and arrogant. Furious, Montezuma struck. Like lightning his front claws slashed out. He had anticipated that his opponent would run; after all that was what usually happened. But his attack was met head on, and the two grappled together, biting and clawing each other in a frenzy of hate. Montezuma knew now that he had underestimated his adversary; he could feel that he was matched for speed and strength, that his every move was parried. As they broke apart again and stood back, a few yards separating them, Montezuma understood that this was to be no ordinary fight. He was already hurt badly, his good ear torn and bleeding. It was a challenge to his supremacy; lose this and he would have no kingdom. For the first time since he was a kitten, Montezuma feared defeat; for the first time in his life he felt tired and shaken.

Both now watched for the other's move, their tails swishing in anger, each trying to outdo the threats of the other. But unlike the black cat, Montezuma was thinking all the time, working out his tactics. He knew he must take the initiative if he was to survive. The standoff lasted some time until both cats had regained their composure, but still neither would leave the field. They skirmished spasmodically, neither inflicting serious damage, but it was after one of these incidents that Montezuma yelled in pain and deliberately turned away and ran – but not too fast. The black cat gave chase as he had hoped and within seconds was on him. Montezuma flipped over onto his back before the teeth could bite and as he did so he found the black cat's throat exposed and unguarded. The bite was accurate and incisive. He felt the grip on him loosen and knew from the cry of pain that the bite had been well placed. The black cat half ran, half shuffled out of the yard and away into the fields. The feint had worked as planned, but at a cost; the ear already torn had been bitten again and the blood flowed freely from the wound.

Matthew found him only by chance late that evening when he came into the yard to grease up the mower. Montezuma was lying by the water trough, blood still pouring from his ear. Not far away was a dead fledgling pigeon up against the barn wall. The cat looked more dead than alive, his eyes were glazed and his breath shallow.

"Loss of blood, more than anything," said the vet after he had patched him up and injected him. "He should pull through, but he'll have matching crumpled ears now. Looks to me as if he came off worse this time. Fights a lot, does he?"

"Yes," said Matthew, stroking the wounded warrior, "But he always wins."

"Didn't do so well this time," Matthew's father said.

"He's getting on, you know," Matthew said defensively. "Not as quick as he was, perhaps. But there's not a cat to touch him." Matthew felt almost personally insulted by this supposition that Montezuma might have lost a fight.

"Past his prime," said his father. "He'll not come through many more like that."

"Maybe the other one's worse off," said Matthew. "We don't know, do we?"

"Well he couldn't be very much worse off than Monty is now, could he?" Matthew's father had to have the last word and it seemed to be fair comment. Montezuma lay there in his basket by the stove scarred and panting; but as they all watched him, the panting turned to the deep roaring self-satisfied purr they all knew.

"What's he purring for?" said Matthew's mother. "He's no right to purr, he's practically dead."

"I bet the other cat isn't purring," said Matthew.

The Seventh Life

Montezuma's boundaries extended as the years passed. He was satisfied as a young cat to roam close to home, returning regularly to the farmhouse for his meal. His favourite hunting grounds lay in the hedges, barns and fields around the farm. Here hunting was a science, and with his knowledge of the ground and his wide experience he could be assured of at least some kind of kill. Beyond, out in the wilderness, hunting was a more chancy affair, and though often more exciting was invariably less successful.

But there was another reason besides hunting for wandering abroad. The local she-cats had become few and far between, and a tom cat must chase the she-cats if he is any kind of tom. Already Montezuma had sired perhaps a hundred kittens during his lifetime. Innumerable tabby farm cats, Persian cats, Siamese cats and once a sleek, aristocratic Abyssinian, all had fallen for his rough charm and the parish was heavily populated with his progeny, many of whom possessed the tell-tale white patch on their throats. His success rate with the ladies merely spurred Montezuma to greater efforts and he began to wander further and further afield in his search for new mates. It was during one of these expeditions that Montezuma over-reached himself and came to grief.

As the years passed, Matthew was taking more and more of the running of the farm onto his own shoulders. It was corn harvest and he had been busy combining the barley and bringing in the bales of straw. With his father and mother he had spent all his waking hours out in the corn fields taking full advantage of a succession of blazing warm days. Every day's harvest was an emergency in case the weather broke before the next day, and they worked late every evening bringing in the sacks and straw before the night came down. There was no time in all this to notice the cat; and so for two or three days no-one realised that Montezuma was missing. By that time Montezuma was a long way away and in deep trouble.

Montezuma had never before ventured beyond the wide main road that cut through the hills several miles from the farm. He lay now in the long grass high above the road and watched the traffic flash by. His ears were back and his heart beat fast: this was not for him. He had been here often enough on previous expeditions and surveyed the unexplored territory on the far side of the road, but always his better judgement had ruled him. This time however Montezuma had been following the scent of a she-cat, and the trail led him like a magnet down the steep slopes towards the edge of the road. This time he had to cross, he had to go on.

The road was a dual carriageway separated by a long strip of grass and shrubby trees. Montezuma took his time, judging all the while the speed of the cars as they approached. For several minutes he watched, his head turning this way and that like an irregular metronome until he was sure that the nearest car was far enough for the attempt to be made. His mind now made up, he sprang out into the road and skipped across, the tarmac hot under his paws. He reached the island with only seconds to spare, springing up from the road into the sanctuary of the dusty grass. It was as he landed that he cut himself. As his back legs came down under him he felt a sharp stabbing pain in one of his rear paws. On three legs he hobbled into the shadow of a thorn bush and lay down to assess the damage. Cautious licking revealed a long gash right across the central pad of his paw. He cleaned it thoroughly and then lay back in the shade to wait for the bleeding to stop.

By late afternoon he was ready to move on, but the expedition into the unknown lands on the other side of the road had had to be abandoned. His one thought now was to get home to the safety of his farmhouse. He limped back through the grass to the edge of the road carrying his injured paw well off the ground and began the long wait for a sufficient pause in the flow of the traffic. The pauses came and went, but the cat was unable to move. Each time he decided to wait for the next opportunity, and then the next and the next. His confidence was disappearing. With only three legs at his disposal his ability to calculate the risk had been upset. Once he did start out to make the crossing but he found he could not gather up enough speed to make it in time. Half way across, his nerve failed him and he turned and scampered back to the island. There he lay down again, dejected, and nursed his throbbing foot. On either side of him the cars and lorries thundered by in an interminable, unbroken procession; and as the evening came on the traffic seemed to intensify. Montezuma lay besieged on his island, hunger, fear and the loss of blood combining to make him tremble from head to foot. He was now totally confused and disorientated. He needed help, so he called out for it; but his yowling was obliterated by the roar of the engines and the continuous swish of the tyres on the soft tarmac.

Sergeant-Major Sydney Shannon hated roads and avoided them whenever he could, but this one lay across his path and had to be crossed. 'Old Syd' as he was known whenever he went in this part of the country, was a country tramp. He had long since given up on the world of people and rarely spoke to anyone unless he had to. His life was spent in the woods and fields deep in the countryside where men had not yet overrun the land completely. Here there was still the quiet to listen to and the space to wander. But even here the roads had come slicing through his fields. He regarded them as an intrusion, an invasion of his privacy, and the people who used them as marauding lemmings. He viewed them with a degree of detached pity and considerable contempt.

Holding up his hand like a policeman he strode out towards the island in the middle of the road, his kitbag over his shoulder. For hundreds of yards back the cars squealed to a halt and set up an indignant honking of horns that Old Syd ignored completely. As he approached the island at his regular unhurried pace, he spied a cat in the grass not more than a few yards from him. Oblivious to the abuse of the drivers behind him, Old Syd unloaded the kit bag from his shoulder and held out his hand towards the cat.

Montezuma's first instinct was to run, for it was a strange looking being that confronted him. Old Syd was a tall man with a craggy, pitted face and a shock of completely white hair that fell down over his forehead. He wore what he always wore, summer or winter, his old heavy khaki trousers over a pair of high black boots, and a drill khaki shirt done up at the neck. His greatcoat was in his pack along with his billycan and his razor.

"Don't be afeared, son," he said. "'Tis only Old Syd and he'll not hurt you. Don't you be afeard."

The voice was warm and gentle, and Montezuma felt he had found a friend. He made no resistance as the old man knelt down beside him and made to stroke his head. The cat stood up, walked towards him and pushed his head into the welcoming hand. "A bad paw, have you, son? We'll soon have that right, soon as we get out of this place. No use waiting for them, son. They never stop. They don't stop for people, so they'd hardly stop for a cat. They'd run you down first and then say sorry after. They're all

in such a hurry." He picked the cat up in his hands and opened the end of his kit bag. "You stay there now, and just watch." With one arm around his kit bag Old Syd stepped out in front of the traffic and threw up his hand in an imperious gesture. He stood, legs apart, in the middle of the road facing the cars until everything had come to a halt. "That's the way to do it, son," he said. "That's the only way." And he turned and walked slowly across the road. Once on the other side he gave the angry motorists a mocking, courtly bow and then climbed the fence into the field beyond. "It must be this way you live," he said. "The other way's all people, and no cat in his right mind wants to be with people."

For a few days after he realised that Montezuma was missing, Matthew did not worry unduly. He had known Montezuma now for nearly ten years and had become convinced of his ability to survive anything; but after a week or so even his conviction began to weaken. He would call for him at all corners of the farm where he was working, and he would ask anyone he met whether they had seen a battered looking ginger tom with a white throat. At home he tried hard to disbelieve his father's pessimism.

"There's any number of ways for a cat to die, any number," said his father. "And he's not immortal you know."

"He'll come back one day, you'll see," said Matthew, but even as he spoke he knew he was deceiving himself.

"Cars, lorries, traps, drowning, poisoning – there's a lot of danger out there for a wandering tom. Even a fox you know, he'll take an old cat if there's nothing else." His father shook his head. "I shouldn't hope too much, if I were you. 'Tis never worth it. Accept the worst, that's what I say."

"He's not that old, Dad," said Matthew.

"And I'll not believe Monty's dead till I see his body for myself."

The days came and went, and stretched into weeks and still Montezuma did not come home. Now even Matthew had to face the probability that Montezuma was dead. No one talked of him any more in the house; even Matthew's father refrained from further speculation. Speculation now led always to the same conclusion, and that they kept private so that each should not reveal his worst misgivings to the other.

After three weeks Matthew's mother moved the cat-box from the corner by the stove and took it out to burn it in the orchard. Matthew noticed it was gone that evening, but he passed no comment. None was needed.

Some miles away in the water meadows that ran alongside the river, the old man and the cat had set up home in a deserted fishing hut. Montezuma's paw had healed cleanly and he spent his convalescence sunning himself on the banks while Old Syd fished for trout in the river. They lived on a diet of trout and milk. The milk was taken surreptitiously from a dreamy Jersey cow that grazed on a hill of buttercups nearby. She stood quite still, only occasionally turning a mildly enquiring eye to see what was going on underneath her. Old Syd talked to her all the while as he filled up his water flask with warm milk. The trout were just as easy for the old man. He made his own flies from the cat's ginger fur and found discarded hooks hanging from the alders along the banks. It was never that long before the line jerked in his hand and he pulled in yet another sparkling trout. No cat would ever leave a diet of fresh trout and warm milk, and Montezuma was no exception.

Every night when he came back from his hunting in the meadows he would find Old Syd awake in the fishing hut, humming in a deep, gruff growl that contained a roll of drums on each note. They were old marching songs and he would hum them over and over again, his arm around the cat. Old Syd was not used to talking to anyone but himself, but now he had

found the perfect audience. The cat would lie by him at night and he would tell him what he had told no other living soul. He would tell of the terrible war he had fought, of the men who had died, of the men he had killed, of the bombing and shooting and the fear. He would tell of his return home to his family, to the street that had crumbled into rubble, to the graves of his wife

and children. He told of the hospital where they thought that he was mad, and the world outside where men still killed each other and where the bombs still fell. The cat lay and purred beside him as he talked, shooting his claws in and out of the greatcoat that acted as a double blanket. "I'd have been happy as a cat," said the old man one evening as he looked down at his companion. "'T'would be good not to know, not to know anything."

A few days later the water bailiff came with a policeman and with the farmer that owned the Jersey cow and the buttercup hill. Old Syd was fishing when he saw them coming. He threw his line in the river and drank down the last drop of the milk. "Trouble," he whispered to the cat. "Seems we've outstayed our welcome. You run along now, son, else they'll pull you in as well, and I shouldn't want that." But that cat sat where he was beside him.

"You again, Syd," said the water bailiff as he came closer. "You've been warned often enough."

"Good afternoon to you as well," said Old Syd.

"Mr. Hildstock here," the policeman said, taking off his cap and wiping his brow. "He says you been at his Miranda."

"Miranda?" Old Syd asked. "Who's Miranda?"

"My cow, that's who," said Mr. Hildstock who had a red face and a jutting chin. "I seen you out there every evening milking her off."

"Only a bit, farmer, only a bit. Only just enough for me and the cat." The old man kicked out to one side at Montezuma. "Go on, son, get out of here, else they'll take you." But the cat ignored him and lay down just out of reach.

"Not on, Syd," said the policeman. "'Tis poaching and theft and we can't have it."

"Don't s'pose you can, son." said Old Syd. "But leave the cat be, he's done nothing. Just leave him be."

"He might belong to someone," said the policeman.

"He doesn't belong to anyone, son; like me. We're the same sort; that's why we get on so well." He bent down and picked up a stone which he threw at the cat. He spoke sharply now for the first time and Montezuma pricked up his ears. "Get out of here, you dumb animal. Can't you see they'll have you too. Get out of here!"

Montezuma ran as the second stone flew past him. He dodged past the farmer who was making a grab for him and made off along the river bank towards the woods.

"Run!" shouted Old Syd. "Run like blazes!" and he cheered as the cat disappeared into the trees. "You'll not get him now, you'll not get him," he said, "but I'm ready for you. Just let me get my things."

That same evening the first heavy spot of rain fell after the long harvest drought. The sky fell lower over the farm and turned a translucent lead. The flies vanished suddenly, and dogs everywhere disappeared under tables at the first dull distant rumble of thunder. In the farmhouse the electricity went off as the lightening struck and candles were brought out. Everyone went to bed early that night, there was little else to do; but they were awakened around midnight by a frantic knocking on the door. Matthew was first down. It was Mr. Varley from the end of the lane.

"Sorry to disturb you so late," he said, "but I thought I should tell you soon as I could."

"What is it?" said Matthew, tying up his dressing gown. "Is something wrong?"

"It's your cat, Matthew," he said. "You know you asked me to keep an eye out for him. Well I did, and as I was coming home from the meeting up in the village, I think I found him."

"Montezuma? You found Monty?" His

mother and father had joined Matthew and the three of them spoke almost as one.

"Where is he?" Matthew asked. "Where d'you find him?"

"He's in the car outside," said Mr. Varley. "But I'm afraid he's dead."

"Dead?" Matthew found tears in his eyes for the first time since he was a child. "Not Monty. He's not dead, can't be."

His father pushed by him. "You sure, Mr. Varley? You sure it's him?"

"Looks to be the same cat to me," he said. "I feel sure it is, but it's your cat and you'd know best. You'd best come and look for yourself – that's the only way to be sure."

They shone torches into the boot of the car while the rain lashed down on their backs. "It's him right enough," said Matthew's father. The dead cat was soaked to the skin, his fur matted and dark, but there was no doubt it was a ginger tom with crumpled ears. Matthew picked him up in the blanket he lay in and carried him into the barn adjoining the house. He laid him down gently on the worktable and they all looked again, just to be sure.

"Not been dead long, I shouldn't think," said Mr. Varley. "He was warm when I picked him up. Been knocked down I shouldn't wonder, trying to get home. He's all broken inside. I don't think he suffered."

"That white patch doesn't seem the same," said Matthew. "Looks a lot smaller than Monty's patch to me."

"It's him all right, lad. No question," said his father, his hand on Matthew's shoulder. "No use clutching at straws, not now. It's Montezuma, and you'd best believe it."

"That's him Matthew," said his mother. "I'd know him anywhere. Poor old thing."

Matthew nodded slowly. "I'll bury him tomorrow," he said, covering the cat in the blanket. "I'll bury him out in the orchard and then that will be that."

The Eighth Life

For some days Montezuma waited under cover of the woods for his friend to come back. Each evening at dusk he would emerge from the shadows and make for the fishing hut; it was always deserted and silent. He would sniff around the old fish bones and prowl the fishing bank calling the old man back, but he never came. So it was that one evening he did not return to the woods but instead made his way up through the buttercup field towards the farmstead beyond. After all this was the way they had taken Old Syd.

He approached the buildings cautiously, sneaking through the long grass and the docks and the thistles, all the while taking stock. His nose told him that this was the way his friend had come, but as he came up the lane and into the farmyard the scent vanished totally. He thought for a moment that he should return to the fishing hut by the river. Home, he knew, lay somewhere the other side of that river that he could not cross. He was about to retrace his steps when he heard the sound of singing on the far side of the farmyard wall. Montezuma was hungry – hunting in the woods had not been good, not after a diet of trout and milk – and where there were people there was always the possibility of food. So he decided to take a chance. He bounded up the steps, jumped down into the vegetable garden beyond and then padded through under the broad beans until he came out into the sunlight beyond.

Lily Hildstock was sitting on a swing under an apple tree in the corner of the garden, her head covered by a white hood and a great wooden cross hanging around her neck on a string. She was draped in a long white habit that covered her from head to foot. She sang in rhythm to her swinging, a slow lilting hymn tune that repeated itself every few seconds. On the grass, scattered around the swing lay her pride of little animals: two white rabbits with pink eyes and twitchy noses, a solitary still tortoise, assorted lizards and slow-worms, three shaggy guinea pigs, a hamster and a speckled hen with a broken leg. When she saw the cat stealing across the lawn she sat up on her swing and put her feet down scuffling the swing to a halt.

Montezuma crouched low on the lawn, his eyes fixed on the hamster. His tail whisked gently. But his plans for the hamster were rudely interrupted. The girl in white was coming towards him. "If you come in peace," she said, holding up her hand in a sign of blessing. "If you come in peace, you are welcome. We are all God's creatures and we do not harm one another." At this moment the animals at her feet sensed the presence of the cat. The rabbits scuttled under the nearest shrub, the tortoise lost its head and the guinea pigs rushed back into their box. But the hamster was asleep by the speckled hen and noticed nothing; the lizards and slow-worms froze where they were. "We are all followers of the blessed Saint Francis," said Lily walking slowly towards the cat, who remained crouched and suspicious. A few paces away she knelt down and held out both her hands. "Come, little cat, come and join us. I am Lily, a nun of the Order of Poor Clares, and I will care for you because you are a creature of God. That is what the blessed Clare taught us."

Bemused, but interested, Montezuma remained where he was until the little girl reached him, stroked him and then picked him up in her arms. "There, little cat, you see. We

mean you no harm. You feel thin. We shall feed you. You need shelter. You will live with us. You have been sent to join us and we shall care for you."

Her mother was calling her from the back door. "Supper, Lily, come in for supper now."

"Sister Lily, Reverend Mother. You must call me properly. You are Mother Superior and I am Sister Lily. We agreed." She stroked the cat cradled in her arms and Montezuma responded immediately with his deep roaring purr.

Her mother sighed and cast her eyes to

heaven. "Sister Lily," she said. "Sister Lily, even nuns have to eat. Will you please come into the Convent for supper now."

"Coming, Reverend Mother," Lily said, "but first we've got to feed this poor starving cat. He's come to us for help. Have you got a saucer of milk and some cornflakes?" At this Lily's mother came round the corner and onto the lawn, shielding her eyes against the sun. "Where did you get that?" she said. "Where did it come from? Whose is it?"

"God's," said Lily, "and he came from God. He needs something to eat, Reverend Mother."

"Lily, this has gone far enough. We said that we had enough animals already in the Convent, in the house I mean. There's no room for any more. We agreed."

"Just this one, Reverend Mother. He's old and hungry. God has sent him, I know he has." Lily brought the cat into the kitchen and set him down by a saucer of creamy milk. Montezuma wasted no time, but lapped the saucer clean and then looked up for more.

"That animal will have to go, Lily," said her mother. "You know what your father thinks of cats. He won't have them on the place. And your Aunt Bessie would be horrified. She can't be in the same room with a cat without sneezing.

And I will not become a rest home for battered animals. The cat must go."

"But Reverend Mother . . ." Lily pushed the tears away from her eyes.

"Mummy," said Lily's mother. "I'm your Mummy, not your Mother Superior. This is a farmhouse, not a Convent. Now take off those ridiculous clothes and come to your senses. Your father has told you often enough not to dress up like that. It's not right, not proper. You're carrying this thing too far. Be kind to animals by all means, but remember there are people around as well."

"More's the pity," the girl mumbled quietly, as she pulled off her nun's habit to reveal a Snoopy tee-shirt and blue jeans.

Her mother spoke sharply. "What's that?"

"I said it's a pity, Mum. He's a nice old cat, a gentle cat. We've never had a cat and I've always wanted one. Can't we keep him, please? He won't be a nuisance. I'll look after him. It'll be the last one, I promise, the very last one."

"No." Her mother took her by the shoulders and shook her. "No, Lily. That cat either belongs to someone, or he's a stray, and he looks more like a stray to me. Now the vet is coming here later on this evening to see Miranda; we'll give it to him and he'll know what to do for the best."

"But you know what he'll do," Lily said. "He'll have him put to sleep. No-one wants an old cat like this, all battered and torn. He'll have him killed, can't you see?"

"If he's not wanted, then that's what's best for him," said her mother, stroking Lily's hair in an effort to console her.

"But he *is* wanted," cried Lily. "I want him."

At this moment Mr. Hildstock and Aunty Bessie came in. She sneezed once and ran out of the door and that was enough to settle the argument for good. Montezuma was wrenched away from his milk and deposited unceremoniously into the bottom of an old corn sack. Mr. Hildstock tied the top firmly, and dumped him out in the old cartshed to await the vet's visit.

Back in the house Mr. Hildstock blamed it all on the old tramp who had been trespassing on his land. "Every year he comes; he leaves dirt wherever he goes. You wash yourself properly, my girl. And don't go round picking up mangy old cats. I've told you before, cats are dirty things. That old man, he steals my fish, steals my milk, infects my Miranda and now he leaves his filthy cat wandering around my farm."

"He's not filthy," shouted Lily. She turned around from the sink and screamed at her father, tears pouring down her face. "He's a kind old cat and Syd's a kind old man. Everyone says so.

He's never done you any harm. You sent for the police and you had Old Syd put in prison and now you're sending away his old cat and he'll be killed. I'll pray for that cat every night till I die, and then God will look after him in Heaven and he'll be there when I get there. Only you won't see him – you'll be in Hell with all the other murderers." Of course she was sent to her room where she flung herself on her bed and prayed. She prayed for the cat's life to be spared and went on praying till the tears stopped flowing and she was left only with a terrible still anger against her father. It was while she was upstairs that the vet came, treated the cow and took away the cat. Lily never saw him again.

Out in the yard before he drove off, the vet peered into the sack in the boot of his car. "Seen that one before somewhere," he said to Mr. Hildstock. "Seen him somewhere, sure I have."

"Only an old stray," Mr. Hildstock said. "Should be put away. Too many like that just running wild. You'll never find a home for him, not at his age."

"Not likely, I agree," said the vet. "Looks a bit of an old warhorse to me. I've a few more calls to make, then I'll take him to the R.S.P.C.A. in town. They'll keep him for a day or two and if he's not claimed they'll put him down. Sure you wouldn't like to keep him? Good mouser by the look of him."

But Mr. Hildstock was already walking away. "No mice on my farm," he said. "There's no mice, so we don't need a cat. He'd be no use here. He's all yours."

Matthew knew there was something wrong as soon as Emma calved. Normally a cow will stand up to lick her calf over immediately after birth, but Emma just lay where she was on the straw and refused to get up. No amount of gentle persuasion or pulling would get her to move and Matthew called his father in to help.

"I think it's that milk fever again," said Matthew.

"We've had a lot of it recently. You see if you can get her up. I've tried everything I know."

His father pulled the new-born calf round to where the cow could see it. "Come on, old girl. She's yours and you got to look after her." But Emma turned away and stared steadfastly in another direction. Then between them they used force, trying to rock the cow up on to her feet, but Emma weighed over half a ton and was not co-operating. Matthew's father stood back and took off his flat cap. "Gad, you're right," he said. "That milk fever, 'tis the divil itself. It's a vet's job. You better have him in quick. If he's not here fast we'll lose that cow and the calf as well as likely as not."

They contacted the vet by radio phone a few minutes after he'd left Mr. Hildstock's farm. They said it was an emergency and that there was no time to lose. A quarter of an hour later he came down the farm track in a cloud of dust and went straight into the shippen to examine the cow. Matthew and his father had been right, it was diagnosed as milk fever; and the vet went back to his car for the syringe. Matthew waited with Emma. "Got to get you up," he said. "You've got to get on with it, you know. That calf of yours needs the milk and you've not given him anything yet. And it was a bull calf again. I've told you often enough, it's heifers we want here. You're an inconvenient sort of cow, but I want you to live. So get up."

"Still talking to them?" said the vet as he came back into the shippen with Matthew's father. "It's not a talk she needs, it's this. A nice drop of calcium and she'll be well on her way."

And so she was. It was not long before Emma was on her feet with her calf suckling frantically underneath her. "Go to it, son," said the vet, packing his bag and rolling down his sleeves. "You're luckier than some I've seen today."

"What d'you mean?" said Matthew.

"Nothing," said the vet. "Nothing. It's just

that I like to see results. I spend far too much of my time putting animals to sleep. I'm just off now into town to the R.S.P.C.A. – another stray. I've never got used to it and I've been at it now for five years. Perhaps I'm in the wrong job."

"No you're not, lad," said Matthew's father. "No you're not. You've saved that cow and I can think of many more you've put to rights for us. You stay put."

"Nice when it works out," said the vet as he started up his car. He had already driven out of the yard gate when Matthew suddenly started shouting and tore up the lane after him waving his hands. The vet spotted Matthew in the driving mirror and screeched to a dusty halt. Matthew came running up and leant on the car door.

"Stray, you said."

"What's that, Matthew?" The vet turned off his engine.

"Stray. You said you had a stray. Stray what?"

"Just a cat," said the vet. "Just an old tom found wandering up on old Hildstock's farm. Why? You wouldn't want a cat, would you? You've got one already, haven't you?"

"He's dead," said Matthew. "Run over a few days ago on the road to the village."

"Oh, I'm sorry, Matthew, sorry to hear that. Would you like a look at this one? He's old, but he looks a tough old devil. He'd be good value on your farm I should think, and I know he'd be a lot better off here than where he's bound for."

"What colour is he?" Matthew asked as the vet tried to undo the string around the top of the sack.

"Don't know, difficult to see in the bottom of a sack, but I'd say he was a gingery sort of a cat with crumpled ears. I've seen him somewhere before, sure I have. I can't get this confounded cord loose."

Matthew gripped his arm. "Did you say ginger?" The vet nodded. "With crumpled ears?"

"Think so."

"But Monty had crumpled ears, and he's ginger."

"Monty?" The vet was looking perplexed.

"My old cat," said Matthew.

'But you said your cat was dead; run over, you said." The vet finally loosened the cord and pulled open the sack. "See for yourself, Matthew, but watch his claws. He doesn't like being in that sack; he's scratched me once today already."

As Matthew looked into the sack, his father

came puffing up the lane and reached the car. "It's him," Matthew said, looking up at the vet and beaming. "It's Monty."

"Monty's dead," said Matthew's father. "We buried him last week. It can't be him."

"He was dead," said Matthew as he pulled Montezuma out of the sack. "He was dead and I buried him, but now he's alive again." He held Montezuma up in the air and examined the white patch on the throat. "I thought so. I knew that patch wasn't the same on the other cat." He set Montezuma down on the ground and crouched down beside him to stroke him.

"Matthew," said the vet. "You're not making much sense."

"He is," said Matthew's father. "Gad, the boy's right, that's Monty back from the dead."

"It's quite simple," said Matthew. "I buried the wrong cat."

"But this one was found over ten miles away on Hildstock's land," said the vet. "He'd been living with an old tramp, or that's what I was told."

Montezuma sat where he was in the dust for a few moments, his eyes still blinded by the bright sun. He looked all around him and up at Matthew to be quite sure that the voice really did belong to the person he had remembered. It did.

At that very moment Sam came up behind the car. The cat's back arched instinctively and then relaxed and the two approached each other and stood nose to nose. The three men looked on as the two animals checked each other over and came to full recognition. For the first time in his life Montezuma brushed himself up against the dog, his tail trembling with affection. Sam looked askance at this and his ears went back, but he stood his ground as the cat wound its way in and out of his legs, purring ecstatically.

"That's the only cat Sam can live with," said Matthew.

"Same as me," said Matthew's father. "There's not another cat I'd have in my house, I can tell you that."

"Then that was the one I fixed up after that dog fight a few years back," said the vet.

"Same cat," said Matthew. "Same dog."

Montezuma was hungry again. He looked up and saw his back door and did not wait to be invited. He bounded down the path and disappeared inside. Matthew and his father waited for the scream of delight they knew would follow. It came a few moments later and Matthew's mother came out of the door shouting to the whole world that she had found Monty, that Monty had come back.

"I'm pleased I came today," said the vet.

"So am I," said Matthew. "So am I."

The End

The seasons on the farm came and went and over the years the world around Montezuma changed. By the time Matthew had married and brought his wife, Zoe, home to live, Montezuma was already an old cat, nearly fourteen years old by Matthew's reckoning, "Love me, love my cat," Matthew had warned her, so Zoe had no option. It was not hard to love Montezuma. Crumpled, slow and dignified there was the look of the old soldier about him that commanded respect and affection.

As the years passed and his powers declined, Montezuma came to live more and more in the farmhouse. With his eyes dimming and his joints stiffening, his hunting days were clearly over; the mice moved too fast and the birds always saw him coming. He could still manage beetles, spiders and leaves but there was little satisfaction there for an old campaigner like Montezuma and

even less nourishment. He came to rely completely on the three meals that Matthew's father prepared for him every day: soggy cornflakes and milk, scraps from the lunch table and a gleaming mackerel every evening. The two grew old together and a bond of great sympathy grew up between them as the years went by. The long sofa in the sitting room was now the resting place for the "two old age pensioners", as Matthew referred to them. They would lie down together during the long afternoon, each reflecting on their early days.

Montezuma had only blurred and indistinct

recollections for the most part, but he thought often about the old man he had lived with in the fishing hut so many years before, of his entombment in the snow; and about Sam, the old sheep dog, now dead and gone and replaced by an ill-mannered puppy who had none of Sam's diplomatic forebearance and dignity, and who barked ceaselessly whenever he spotted Montezuma. He remembered too the little girl with the long hair whom he had found singing on her swing in the garden. He had his nightmares as well and he could not forget them, but the one that troubled him most, that made him wake up with a start,

was the vision of the great black cat with shining teeth that he had fought in the yard, stalking through the grass towards him.

When Matthew's son was born, it was Montezuma that took over the role of sentry in the shade of the pram in the back yard. He would wait by the back door until Zoe had tucked the baby into his pram. He would watch while she bent over him and listen as the two cooed and gurgled to each other in delight. Then he would take up his post underneath, curl himself up into

a ball and lie there daydreaming until the pram was emptied again. If the baby cried and no-one came he would walk back into the house and yowl until they followed him back outside again. Then, his duty done, he would creep into the sitting room, seek out the softest available patch on the sofa and snuggle down by Matthew's father to finish his dreams.

Only occasionally now did he accompany Matthew out onto the farm and then only as far as the end of the lane. There he would sit and wait in the middle of the road until Matthew came walking back from the milking parlour across the road, the churn swinging in his hand. The waiting was long and he would while away the hours enveloped in the fantasy of his past, trying to forget the pain in his joints and the ache along his back.

Deafness came with old age so that he heard little now of the world around him. It had come on gradually so that he was not aware that he was missing anything. He would sit there in the middle of the road waiting for Matthew, and the tractors and cars would slow down and drive around him. To them he had become an expected hazard, like a pothole in the road that you have to avoid. Everyone in the lane knew Montezuma, and everyone took great care not to disturb him. On his part he never paid the cars any attention but sat neat and upright, his eyes closed waiting for Matthew to come back. But as everyone said, shaking their heads, one day someone would come who did not know that the crossroads belonged to Montezuma.

The holiday season brought strange cars down the lane, packed with lively children, yapping dogs and picnic baskets. When the sun shone warm and strong from deep blue skies then the people came out of hibernation from miles around, came down the road past farm lane and made for the shady banks of the river.

Often enough Mr. Varley had emerged from his cottage at the crossroads, picked Montezuma up and put him down in the safety of the hedge-row. "It's dangerous to be there, my dear," he'd say. "Not a place for an old cat like you. I'll park you by the hedge here, and you can wait for Matthew to come back. He won't be long." But he was long and Montezuma very soon crept out of the hedge and moved out into the middle of the road again where he could see further round the bend in the direction Matthew always came from.

That dusty September evening, many cars had passed him safely enough, until at dusk a big black car with rows of shining chrome like teeth came rushing towards him. The family inside was noisy after the excitement of their picnic and the father turned round in fury to silence the riot on the back seat. It needed only that one momentary distraction, and the car was on top of the cat before he had time to hit his brake. Montezuma had opened his eyes, feeling the vibration in the road underneath him. He sensed there was danger and would have moved, but hesitated for just one split second. The car was from his nightmare. Could he still be dreaming? Was this the black cat coming for him again.? He tried to move at the last moment but his legs were stiff and would not obey him quickly enough. The car hit him on the side as he sprang away and bowled him into the ditch. When he tried to right himself he found his back legs would not respond, they had gone quite numb and useless. He lay back and waited for his strength to return. When he looked up there were faces peering down at him.

"Is he dead?"

"Only an old cat."

"I never even saw him."

"Only an old farm cat. His eyes are open. He's alive. He'll be all right."

"Shouldn't we tell someone?"

"It'll only upset the children, you know that. And we're late as it is."

"But we can't just leave him there."

"What else can we do? He's just a tatty old farm cat – plenty more where he came from."

"D'you think he's bad? D'you think he'll live?"

"Course he will. Tough as old boots they are. He's just stunned, that's all. Nine lives they've got, remember?"

The children kept calling from the car and that settled the matter. The car drove off and the lane was silent again. Montezuma summoned all his tired strength and pulled himself along the ditch, up through a hole in the hedge and away towards the farm across the barley fields.

Later that evening, when Montezuma had not returned for his evening meal, the family went out looking. Montezuma hadn't gone missing like this for years and they all feared the worst. Matthew's mother and father searched the farm buildings near the house whilst Matthew and Zoe combed the fields and hedgerows down towards the river and along the road. Mr. Varley came out when he heard them calling and joined in the search. No-one rested until it was too dark to go on and even then Matthew stayed outside calling in the silence of the night.

He didn't know what made him climb the bales in the big barn, but he had often found Montezuma lying asleep up under the warm corrugated roof on a bed of soft hay. He had already searched the stack once without success. However, this time he climbed to the very topmost layer up amongst the rafters. He shone his torch into the darkest corners of the stack, sweeping systematically around him in ever decreasing arcs. The beam came to rest at the end of a row of broken bales. He hoped it was an old sack, but knew inside himself that he had found Montezuma.

He was lying stretched out in a deep bed of hay. His two back legs were twisted awkwardly and the head hung loose, the eyes closed. It was quite obvious he was dead.

He buried the old cat that same night by torch-light, marking the place in the spinney with the spade. When he went into the house he told no-one, but went straight to bed. He hadn't the stomach to break the news. That night he lay awake thinking of old Monty and the times they had spent together. He tried to imagine the old cat a kitten once again but could not bring the picture into focus. He kept coming back to the last time he had seen him, sitting out in the lane as he went off down to milking that afternoon. He would not tell the others of the broken back, of what he suspected had happened. He would say he had found him right up on the hay stack, that he had just curled up and died as old cats do, away from everyone and where no one should find them.

It was his father's idea to dig up a young oak sapling and to plant it over Montezuma's grave. They stood back once it was done while Zoe planted a few daffodil bulbs in the soft earth around the tree.

"That'll be there longer'n me," said Matthew's father, "and longer'n any of us. It'll grow fine and strong like Monty. Come on then," he said, turning away abruptly. "Can't be wasting time. There's that hedge down along the road that needs laying again, Matthew. The sheep'll be breaking out there before the end of the winter if you're not careful. Can't stand around here all day. There's work to be done."

A few nights later, high up amongst the soft warm hay in the old barn, a young she-cat gave birth to her first litter of kittens. There were three, and one of them was ginger with a great white patch on his throat.